F

by Harry Conroy

LangSyne
PUBLISHING
WRITING *to* REMEMBER

LangSyne
PUBLISHING
WRITING to REMEMBER

79 Main Street, Newtongrange,
Midlothian EH22 4NA
Tel: 0131 344 0414 Fax: 0845 075 6085
E-mail: info@lang-syne.co.uk
www.langsyneshop.co.uk

Design by Dorothy Meikle
Printed by Ricoh Print Scotland

ISBN 978-1-85217-089-9

Forbes

SEPT NAMES INCLUDE:

Bannerman
Berry
Boyes
Fordyce
Lumsden
Mekie
Middleton
Walters
Watson
Watt
Wattie

Forbes

MOTTO:
Grace Me Guide.

CREST:
A Stag's Head Proper.

TERRITORY:
Aberdeenshire.

Chapter one:

The origins of the clan system

by Rennie McOwan

The original Scottish clans of the Highlands and the great families of the Lowlands and Borders were gatherings of families, relatives, allies and neighbours for mutual protection against rivals or invaders.

Scotland experienced invasion from the Vikings, the Romans and English armies from the south. The Norman invasion of what is now England also had an influence on land-holding in Scotland. Some of these invaders stayed on and in time became 'Scottish'.

The word clan derives from the Gaelic language term 'clann', meaning children, and it was first used many centuries ago as communities were formed around tribal lands in glens and mountain fastnesses.

The format of clans changed over the centuries, but at its best the chief and his family held the land on behalf of all, like trustees, and the ordinary clansmen and women believed they had a blood relationship with the founder of their clan.

There were two way duties and obligations. An inadequate chief could be deposed and replaced by someone of greater ability.

Clan people had an immense pride in race. Their relationship with the chief was like adult children to a father and they had a real dignity.

The concept of clanship is very old and a more feudal notion of authority gradually crept in.

Pictland, for instance, was divided into seven principalities ruled by feudal leaders who were the strongest and most charismatic leaders of their particular groups.

By the sixth century the 'British' kingdoms of Strathclyde, Lothian and Celtic Dalriada (Argyll) had emerged and Scotland, as one nation, began to take shape in the time of King Kenneth MacAlpin.

Some chiefs claimed descent from

ancient kings which may not have been accurate in every case.

By the twelfth and thirteenth centuries the clans and families were more strongly brought under the central control of Scottish monarchs.

Lands were awarded and administered more and more under royal favour, yet the power of the area clan chiefs was still very great.

The long wars to ensure Scotland's independence against the expansionist ideas of English monarchs extended the influence of some clans and reduced the lands of others.

Those who supported Scotland's greatest king, Robert the Bruce, were awarded the territories of the families who had opposed his claim to the Scottish throne.

In the Scottish Borders country – the notorious Debatable Lands – the great families built up a ferocious reputation for providing warlike men accustomed to raiding into England and occasionally fighting one another.

Chiefs had the power to dispense justice

and to confiscate lands and clan warfare produced a society where martial virtues – courage, hardiness, tenacity – were greatly admired.

Gradually the relationship between the clans and the Crown became strained as Scottish monarchs became more orientated to life in the Lowlands and, on occasion, towards England.

The Highland clans spoke a different language, Gaelic, whereas the language of Lowland Scotland and the court was Scots and in more modern times, English.

Highlanders dressed differently, had different customs, and their wild mountain land sometimes seemed almost foreign to people living in the Lowlands.

It must be emphasised that Gaelic culture was very rich and story-telling, poetry, piping, the clarsach (harp) and other music all flourished and were greatly respected.

Highland culture was different from other parts of Scotland but it was not inferior or less sophisticated.

Central Government, whether in London

"The spirit of the clan means much to thousands of people"

or Edinburgh, sometimes saw the Gaelic clans as a challenge to their authority and some sent expeditions into the Highlands and west to crush the power of the Lords of the Isles.

Nevertheless, when the eighteenth century Jacobite Risings came along the cause of the Stuarts was mainly supported by Highland clans.

The word Jacobite comes from the Latin for James – Jacobus. The Jacobites wanted to restore the exiled Stuarts to the throne of Britain.

The monarchies of Scotland and England became one in 1603 when King James VI of Scotland (1st of England) gained the English throne after Queen Elizabeth died.

The Union of Parliaments of Scotland and England, the Treaty of Union, took place in 1707.

Some Highland clans, of course, and Lowland families opposed the Jacobites and supported the incoming Hanoverians.

After the Jacobite cause finally went down at Culloden in 1746 a kind of ethnic cleansing took place. The power of the chiefs was curtailed. Tartan and the pipes were banned in law.

Many emigrated, some because they wanted to, some because they were evicted by force. In addition, many Highlanders left for the cities of the south to seek work.

Many of the clan lands became home to sheep and deer shooting estates.

But the warlike traditions of the clans and the great Lowland and Border families lived on, with their descendants fighting bravely for freedom in two world wars.

Remember the men from whence you came, says the Gaelic proverb, and to that could be added the role of many heroic women.

The spirit of the clan, of having roots, whether Highland or Lowland, means much to thousands of people.

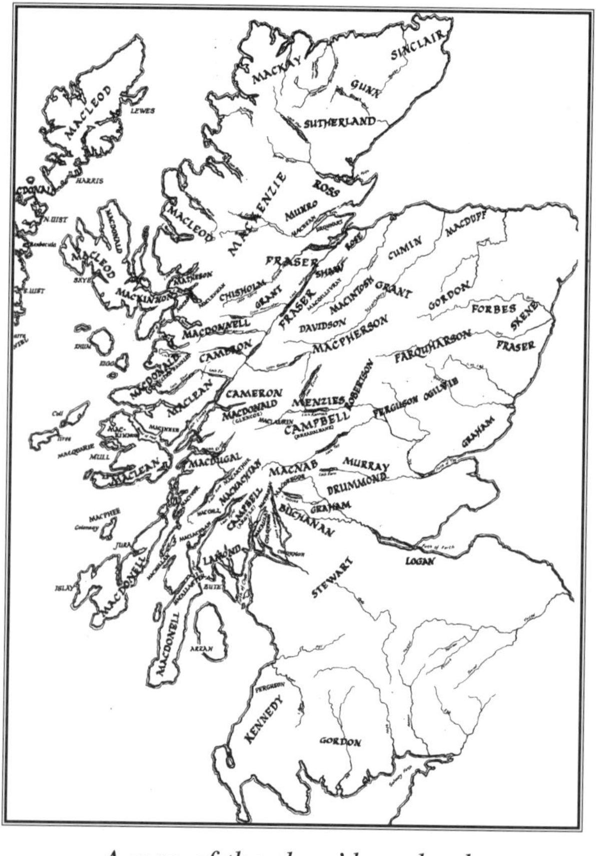

A map of the clans' homelands

Chapter two:

Lords of Donside

The verdant territories of the redoubtable Clan Forbes spread broadly over the western hinterlands of Aberdeenshire, chiefly along the meandering banks of the sparkling River Don.

Here the great houses, estates and castles of the clan proliferated – at one time there were more than 150 such grand structures.

Many are renowned for their gothic, baronial architecture and even those that are ruined remain forbidding and atmospheric.

Castle Forbes, built in 1815 (the year of Waterloo) by James Ochonar, 17th Lord Forbes, still stands, proud and defiant, overlooking the Don, occupied by the direct descendants of Duncan Forbes upon whom the original lands were conferred in a charter dated 1271 by King Alexander III.

The clan name was originally pronounced as two syllables and comes from the

Gaelic *forba* meaning field or district which was also the name given to a parish in rural Aberdeenshire.

Tradition relates how the founder of the clan, Oconachar, killed a ferociously predatory bear which had devoured nine maidens at the well that still commemorates their savage demise.

Oconachar then took proud possession of the Braes of Forbes which the beast had previously made uninhabitable.

John de Forbes fought alongside Bruce in the Wars of Scottish Independence against Edward I; and his son, Sir Christian de Forbes, successfully defended Urquhart Castle on Loch Ness against a besieging English army.

The family power was increased throughout the medieval period.

Sir John Forbes of the Black Lip had four sons in the fourteenth century: William became the progenitor of the Pitsligo line; John was the ancestor of the Polquhoun line; Alistair of Brux founded the lines of Skellater and Inverernan; while Alexander, the eldest, fought in the victory at Harlaw in 1411 alongside the Earl of Mar against the invading hordes led by Donald of the Isles, and was elevated to the peerage, taking his seat in Parliament.

Since then the title has been handed down through successive generations; and on the union role of 1701, the title of Forbes was the premier Lordship of Scotland, a precedence held to this day.

James, the son of the 1st Lord Forbes, also had three sons: William became the 3rd Lord Forbes; Duncan founded the Corsindae and Monymusk lines; while Patrick of Corse, squire to King James III, founded the line which later provided the Baronets of Craigievar.

Throughout the fifteenth and sixteenth centuries, a long, bitter and bloody struggle was waged against the neighbouring great house of Gordon, a feud which claimed many victims over succeeding, increasingly violent, decades.

Murders were commonplace and the blood vendettas spread throughout the north-east so that the Forbes clan had an increasing array of enemies, including the Leslies, the Irvines, the Setons and the Earls of Huntly who led the Gordon faction.

Religion was added to the brew because, after the Reformation, the Forbes clan were rigorously Protestant while the Gordons remained defiantly Catholic.

Huntly became involved in a plot aimed at discrediting the Master of Forbes, son of the 6th Lord, who had been involved in the murder of one of his close allies, Seton of Meldrum.

In 1536, Huntly, gathering bogus evidence, accused Forbes of conspiring to assassinate King James V by shooting at him with a cannon.

The Master was duly tried and beheaded: but within days his conviction was reversed and the Forbes family was restored to favour (but too late for the wrongly accused victim of the plot).

However, the damage done to relations between the rival clans was immense and for the remainder of the sixteenth century Aberdeenshire was reduced to a state of bloodstained anarchy.

The allies of the Clan Forbes – all Protestants – were Keiths, Frasers and Crichtons.

The feud culminated in 1571 in two ferocious but indecisive battles at Tillieangus and Craibstone. There were many casualties but no real winners.

Meanwhile, Druminnor, then the seat of Lord Forbes, was plundered and set on fire; while the Gordons went on to massacre 27 Forbeses of Towie at Corgarff Castle (also incinerated).

Two Acts of Parliament had to be passed to force the clans to lay down their arms and make an uneasy peace, though it took several generations for the feuding to completely die out.

Chapter three:

On both sides

Though the Clan Forbes was traditionally Protestant, Covenanting and Whig, they were represented on both sides during the Jacobite rebellions.

Alexander Forbes of Pitsligo, fiery and unpredictable, supported both the 1715 and 1745 Rebellions; and it says much for clan loyalty that, a hunted rebel, he was able to hide out on Donside for years with a price on his head.

On one occasion he was actually saved by a Gordon, an elderly spinster who hid him behind her bed. When the redcoats felt her body to make sure she was not a man, she had to cough loudly to drown out Pitsligo's heavy breathing nearby.

The Rev. Robert Forbes of Leith collected an invaluable group of anecdotes about the '45 Rebellion under the heading *The Lion In Mourning*: but the most important figure at this

troubled time was Duncan Forbes of Culloden who belonged to a branch of the Forbeses of Tolquhon.

A lawyer and politician, he was eventually created Lord President of the Court of Session (the country's top judge) and became virtually the sole representative of the government in the north during the earlier part of the '45.

As such, he was part diplomat, part secret agent, and was instrumental in persuading many clan chiefs not to join up with Bonnie Prince Charlie's forces, thus saving many a family from ruin.

Some historians even claim he was instrumental in saving the Hanoverian throne because if these same powerful chiefs, with their thousands of loyal, warlike followers, had joined the '45 then the result could have been victory for the Jacobites.

The final battle of the campaign, of course, literally took place on his doorstep and he viewed the brief clash – more a massacre than a battle – through his study telescope.

He was the first to despatch reports south to London confirming the complete rout of the Jacobite army: but his brave efforts to restrain the murderous, rampaging redcoats after the battle met with the scorn of their commander 'Butcher' Cumberland who called him 'that old woman' because he kept trying to intercede to save the lives of the vanquished Highlanders.

Chapter four:

The Lonach March

Other branches of the Forbes clan prospered and built some of the finest Scottish tower houses in the land.

The gem was the pink-stoned, fairytale castle of Craigievar, all turrets, spires and parapets, built in 1626 by 'Danzig' Willie Forbes who got his nickname because he was a successful timber merchant who had made his fortune trading in the Baltic. He was a man of taste and sensibility, determined that his keep should be a work of art - which is exactly what it turned out to be. He then furnished it with beautiful paintings, furniture and ornaments and declared that he was one Forbes who had turned his back 'on the old wild life of struggle and strife.'

The massive ruined castle of Tolquhoun near Tarves was built in the 1580s by an ancient branch of the Forbes family who had acquired their land in 1420; while the five towers of Fyvie

Castle, another Forbes stronghold, enshrine five centuries of Scottish history, each built by successive owners. Haunted by a Green Lady and numerous other ghosts, it was bought from the Forbes-Leith family by the National Trust for Scotland and is considered to be the grandest example of Scottish baronial architecture.

Plundered by Highland raiders, Forbes of Corse vowed to build 'such a house as thieves will need to knock at ere they enter!' The result was the splendid Corse Castle erected near Lumphannan in 1581.

A Forbes fought at Custer's Last Stand and is commemorated in St. John's Episcopal Church in Lothian Road in Edinburgh's city centre where an ornate brass wall plaque reads: 'Sacred to the memory of John Stuart Forbes, born Rugby, Warwickshire, 1843 - died June 25th, 1876, with the United States 7th Cavalry.'

His branch of the Forbes clan were a wealthy upper class family who worshipped at St. John's where many of them lie buried.

This particular Forbes was one of those

stereotypes so beloved of Victorian novelists – the upper class rake who causes his ultra-respectable parents all kinds of heartache.

Plagued by gambling debts and wracked with drink, he was forced to emigrate to America and took to heart the exhortation to head west. He ended up joining the cavalry as an ordinary trooper under a false name 'John Hiles'.

Forbes was among the 210 soldiers cut down when 3,000 Sioux and Cheyenne warriors under Crazy Horse wiped out the command of General George Armstrong Custer on the banks of the Little Bighorn River in Montana.

The Indians left Forbes' personal private papers alone; and also his beloved backgammon set was found untouched on the battlefield, an ironic touch as it had been his compulsive gambling that had been one of the root causes for his alienation from his family back home.

This backgammon set and his papers were returned to the clan in Edinburgh who then erected the wall plaque: but the unlucky trooper was not completely forgotten because a mysterious woman in black used to make sporadic visits over from America to place flowers in front of his memorial.

A more successful military Forbes was James Ochoncar, the 17th Lord Forbes, who was an officer in the Coldstream Guards for 26 years, rising to the rank of General. He served as second-in-command to the British forces in Sicily in 1808 before commanding the Cork and Eastern districts in Ireland. It was during this time that a castle was built near Alford on the site of the old family home of Putachie and the 17th Lord is generally regarded as being responsible for the building and layout of this beautiful estate.

Nigel Forbes, the 22nd Lord, followed his father Atholl into the Grenadier Guards and fought throughout the major campaigns of the Second World War before becoming military assistant to the High Commissioner for Palestine, General Sir Alan Cunningham.

Like his father and many earlier holders of the title, Nigel was elected to serve as a representative peer for Scotland in the House of Lords and was Minister of State for Scotland in the Conservative government of Harold Macmillan in the late 1950s.

The martial strain in the clan went way back into the mists of time.

The Forbes chieftain raised 1,000 men for the King in 1594; and in 1628 Lord Forbes agreed to furnish 800 for foreign service; while his son served under Gustavas Adolphus of Sweden and rose to the rank of lieutenant general during the wars against Russia and Turkey. A militant chaplain called William Forbes also earned praise in Adolphus's army for 'having more courage, discretion and good conduct than some captains.'

There were also numerous mercenaries over the centuries who fought in Continental armies, bringing their martial expertise, learned in the north-east glens, to foreign conflicts.

When it comes to the Forbes tartan, unusually there are three versions.

Miss Forbes of Pitsligo is said to have created the most popular one by simply changing the yellow line of the regimental Gordon tartan to white in 1822, thus producing a pattern which is almost identical to the Lamont design.

While the Forbes dress tartan could be taken for the hunting tartan of Cluny Macpherson, the third tartan is similar to that of the Black Watch.

The Forbes clan gathering is held on the last Saturday of each August and a thoroughly memorable occasion it always proves to be.

The Games are held on Donside, of course, and were officialy founded in 1822, though there had been informal gatherings going back centuries.

The Lonach Games, as they are called, are held at Bellabeg Park beside the village of Strathdon.

They are noted for their unique March of the Clansmen which involves around 200 of the Forbes and Wallace families marching with pikes and in full Highland dress behind a pipe band six miles up and down a picturesque glen, stopping at every large house en route (nowadays including the home of Billy Connolly) where trays of double whiskies are served to the marchers.

After a hefty lunch in a local hotel, the marchers then parade around the stadium to open the Games. A horse and cart are conveniently supplied at the rear for any men who may have become overcome by excitement.

These occasions are much more relaxed and friendly than the more posh Royal Braemar Gatherings; and as the Editor of *Scottish Memories* magazine, George Forbes, once memorably wrote in an issue:

'I can personally testify to the thrill, enjoyment and exuberance of these friendly occasions.

'In the crystal blue of an Aberdeenshire summer morning when the skirling pipes echo round the verdant, swirling trees and the drums beat off the purple mountains, something stirs in the blood and you are taken way back to the days when the horizon was limitless and the world was young and nothing mattered.'

Clan warfare produced a society where courage and tenacity were greatly admired

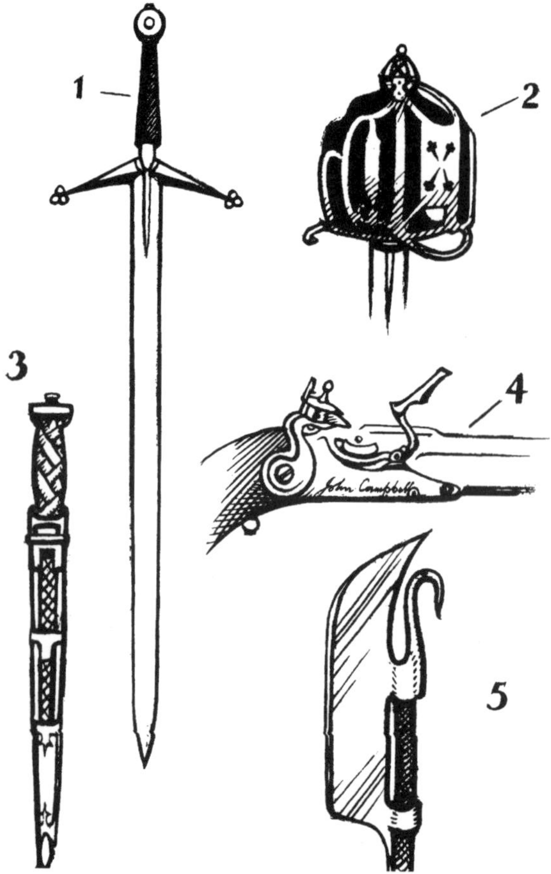
1
2
3
4
John Campbell
5

Highland weapons

1) The claymore or two-handed sword *(fifteenth or early sixteenth century)*

2) Basket hilt of broadsword made in Stirling, 1716

3) Highland dirk *(eighteenth century)*

4) Steel pistol *(detail)* made in Doune

5) Head of Lochaber Axe as carried in the '45 and earlier